BÔ YIN RÂ

THE BOOK ON LOVE

For more information about Bô Yin Râ
and his books available in English translation,
visit The Kober Press web site at
www.kober.com.

BÔ YIN RÂ
(J. A. SCHNEIDERFRANKEN)

THE BOOK ON LOVE

TRANSLATION BY
B.A. REICHENBACH

BERKELEY, CALIFORNIA

For permission to quote or excerpt, write to:
THE KOBER PRESS
2534 Chilton Way
Berkeley, California 94704
email: koberpress@mindspring.com

This book is a translation from the German of the second edition of *Das Buch der Liebe*, published by Kober'sche Verlagsbuchhandlung, Basel-Leipzig in 1931. The first edition of the work was published in 1922 by Verlag der Weißen Bücher, München. The copyright to the German original is held by Kober Verlag, AG, Bern, Switzerland.

Printed in the United States of America

International Standard Book Number: 978-0-915034-12-3

Typesetting and design by Archetype Typography, Berkeley, CA

Book cover after a design by Bô Yin Râ

ACKNOWLEDGMENTS

For their continuing generous support
I gratefully express my indebtedness
to the
Deutsche Bô Yin Râ – Stiftung
Giessen, Germany.

And for her careful readings of
the drafts of this translation
and her many thoughtful comments
I owe sincere thanks to
Alice Glawe

CONTENTS

The first edition of this work
appeared in 1922, four years
after the end of World War I,
at the time called
"The Great War." —Trans.

INTRODUCTION

AT A TIME IN HISTORY when every fertile pasture of mankind is desecrated by befouling tides of hate, the topic I shall speak of in the present book is love.

You, a reader who would find your own eternal self, shall here discover freedom in its highest form.

The freedom that your soul demands, even as your lungs crave air for breathing, only love can ever grant you. And if you are devoid of love you will extinguish in yourself the spark of life from which you are to be reborn anew, unfolding in a growth that in itself is without end.

HERE WE SHALL REFLECT upon a power whose spiritual nature rules all forces on this earth;

a power only very few *experience* in themselves; for while they give the name of "love" to many things, they are too readily contented at that level, without exploring their profoundest depth. But in their inmost depth alone could love reveal to them its radiant might.

Yet only those who in themselves have searched their deepest ground will there as well uncover the foundations of those teachings of celestial love whose wisdom ancient texts of sacred scripture have preserved until this day. Texts that many "know" by heart from having heard and read their words, but whose eternal substance few have grasped in spirit, because they did not realize that in these teachings they receive the revelation of a law that even the most powerful of mortals must obey, if he would not, for all his might, ultimately shatter on his own existence.

If human beings sensed what power love embodies, this planet's face would ages since have undergone a transformation; and life on earth would long ago have freed itself from agonies relentlessly repeated.

The words of sacred wisdom in the ancient texts that touch upon that love remain as darkly veiled today as in the past, and only rare exceptions among seekers have been able, for their own discernment, to draw these veils aside.

What they encountered here no longer was the kind of "love" they knew before; as now they felt a primal cosmic force that sent its shudders through their very bones; a force that made them tremble in their inmost being and freed them to be masters where before they had been slaves.

Such is the love this book would make you come to know.

Such is the love toward which it seeks to guide your soul.

Such is the love whose light imbues the writer's life who in these pages tells you of its power.

Only those whose lives embody timeless love, who know such love from living it as a continuous experience, should have the right to make themselves its witness.

For they alone are truly able to speak of the immeasurable greatness of the power that is here to be discussed.

There have been many who believed their lives informed with love because they were incapable of feeling hate.

This incapacity, however, provides no proof at all that such a person has experienced timeless love.

Hatred is love's polar opposite—the selfsame force inverted—and anyone who cannot hate, while knowing well that feeling hatred is benighted folly, shall likewise never know the kind of love of which St. Paul, in whom its power truly had awakened, bore witness with the words:

"Though I speak with the tongues of men and of angels, and have not love, I am become as sounding brass, or a tinkling cymbal."

Nor will they comprehend the meaning of the legend telling how an adversary of the Shakya-Muni, the Indian Buddha, one day had a raging elephant let loose on the approaching sage's path. But the Enlightened One, to everyone's amazement, tamed the angry animal, so that it trembled as it kneeled before him, conquered by the might of love the sage embodied and had sent against its wrath.

Both the Indian legend and the words of Paul, the "Apostle of the Nations," proclaiming Jesus the Anointed, will let a reader who probes deeper levels recognize that here we are not merely dealing with emotional rapture, but that the authors rather sought to glorify the name of the celestial power that, as I said before, will spiritually master every force on earth.

This power manifests itself in life on earth in many forms.

You find it present in each plant, in every animal, and all of nature's drives of procreation bear witness to its life-embracing force.

But at this level you encounter only its most primitive effects, in which you surely will not at the same time also recognize its most sublime potential; although much more is active even in the former than you until this day may likely have perceived.

Had you ever, even at this lowest rung of love, allowed the searing flames of procreative passion serve you as a witness, and this you truly might have done, you long since would have gained the insight that this primordial energy is capable of generating more than merely mortal human life from earthly human substance.

You then would long ago have also recognized that these all-powerful creative surges must needs be part of love in its sublimest form as well. And thus you would not have embraced the blithe illusion that made you think mere sentiments of gentle sympathy and pious meekness will suffice to turn you into more than what the love-imbued Apostle had dismissed as "sounding brass, or a tinkling cymbal."

All other features the impassioned teacher listed in describing how love in highest form will manifest itself are merely the external signs that will appear wherever love reveals itself in its sublimest nature.

But you mistook these outward attributes of love as being love itself, and now you labor to produce the various qualities within you, which would be yours without all effort, automatically, had love indeed awakened in your being.

I HERE SHALL HAVE TO RID your mind of many misconceptions if I would make you capable of truly knowing love.

Your thoughts are still entangled in delusions, nurtured through millennia, to which you were exposed since early youth.

Those who were appointed to instruct you had themselves heard nothing different from what they passed along to you.

It would be very foolish if you today heaped all your scorn on them.

They merely gave you things they had themselves received; even as I give you now what I had once been given, before I had grown able to draw upon the well of truth myself, employing my own vessel.

Perhaps you will discover that, in the end, it is by no means all the same from which particular well a teacher fills his cup.

If you already are acquainted with the ancient teachings I was granted to present in modern form in other books I published, you also know that what I draw upon are mountain springs that well from ageless rock; and that their waters were the source of every spiritual insight whose disclosure has born fruit on earth through all of human history.

Blest you will be if the *living waters* of that source shall nourish and revive your spirit!

Blest you are if what I have to tell you does not become a "stumblingstone" at which you take "offense," even though I shall be forced to show you that authentic revelation from the Spirit's realm is a continuing, eternal process and that it will itself create, in any age, the witness who shall be its voice.

I CERTAINLY WOULD NOT BE who I am if I intended to devalue any insights in the ancient teachings of religion that ultimately rest upon disclosures made by others of my kind.

And everything that truly bears the Spirit's living seal in all the teachings of the Eastern world, both far and near, had in its day been given by the revelations of those who are my spiritual kindred.

To be sure, my spiritual "genealogy" extends to far more distant ages than the biological heredity of the material human form that is my present instrument, the necessary agent in external life.

Here I mainly would alert you to distinguish very clearly between the Spirit's sanctioned gifts, which those alone are able to convey who are themselves united with the Spirit, but seldom will reveal their nature to the world,—and all the notions that, by contrast, are simply the inflated, sterile phantoms of opinionated minds, equally transmitted in the writings of the ancient peoples, all of which you find mysterious and venerate alike as "holy writ."

How you can learn to differentiate the substance of the ancient texts, my words are meant to show you.

I here instruct you as the only one among my equals in the Spirit who at this time performs his work in public—and as the only human mortal who in this day may claim that he is using words exclusively to serve as vessels of the Spirit's wealth, which is begotten of the Origin.

CHAPTER ONE

THE GREATEST OF COMPASSION'S MEDIATORS

To view the portrait *Jesus Nazarenus*
by Bô Yin Râ visit our web site at
www.kober.com/jesus.htm

If here your eyes are to be opened to the light-begotten power that is love, it is no more than fitting that we should first pay homage to the greatest Mediator of that love among all mortals ever to have lived on earth.

Whether you profess allegiance to his name, or stand apart from the religious creeds that, through the centuries, have risen on the background of his teachings, but often salvage only traces of his sayings, fraught with contradictions, from ruined sites of ancient shrines—you surely will not look upon him with indifference wherever you behold the image of his life reveal the essence of his teachings.

To be sure, the truth about his life has been obscured by many hands, so that today you have but little hope of finding much of what he taught in its authentic form and place, such as the venerated Master once had said it to his pupils.

Yet all distortions notwithstanding, enough survived that still reflects the light of his authentic words. And once you have developed your ability to recognize the genuine sayings in the texts, neither the debris of ancient pagan cults, nor the opinions and beliefs of those who wrote the early records will any longer warp your image of the Master as he truly was.

You merely need to learn how to examine, unencumbered by assumptions, the writings that you are by custom offered as "contemporary" records of a mortal human's life; a man who in his time, was an enigma to his followers, and has remained so to all later generations, even to this day.

BECAUSE ONE DARED NOT touch the ancient texts wherein the teachings, given by the Master through the spoken word, had been reshaped

He rebuked the crowd whose "ears are dull of hearing," a people who has ears in order only "not to hear," and thus was bound to rush into its own undoing.

He long had been aware of how his mortal life would end; yet when the day arrived that forced him to confront that end, all his lofty resolution falters. And, bitterly lamenting, he weeps over Jerusalem, because she had not comprehended, in his day, the revelations he had meant to bring his people.

The few he nonetheless had chosen as his pupils often heard his harsh reproaches "for the hardness of their hearts," and only seldom did he trust their comprehension.

At times he wanted to persuade himself that those who were so faithfully devoted to him in their outer lives, surely must at last have understood him. But then he would discover, once again, with sorrow and compassion, how very far removed their hearts still were from grasping what he taught.

And so he journeyed through the lands of Palestine, teaching in the "schools," the local synagogues, to show the deeper wisdom hidden in the ancient scriptures. He speaks in simple language to the people in order to awaken listeners' hearts. He discloses to his friends the mystery behind his mission, which they fail to comprehend, being too entangled in their nation's messianic fantasies. And thus, despite his every effort, he remains misunderstood by all, but for the one disciple "whom he loved."

He speaks about his "Father," and they assume he means their people's tribal god, disregarding that he most explicitly rejects submission to this "god of vengeance," who had spoken to "the ancients." Indeed, he plainly abrogates that god's supposed "law," when, by virtue of the Spirit's power, he forcefully declares, "But I say unto you . . ."

He speaks of his transcendent mission, and they surmise he meant to reestablish the external power of their earthly state; even though he many times had told them that the realm wherein he was a *king* did not depend for its eternal glory on any might "of this material world."

He speaks of that which in his very self had taken on the form of "flesh and blood," and teaches that the Spirit's life is *physically embodied*. But they misunderstand his words to mean that his material body, born to him on earth, must here become their earthly food, like bread and wine.

Those among the poor whom he was able to relieve of their diseases had faith in him and saw him as a helper in their need. They did not realize, however, that his healing power rested solely in his mortal body and hardly touched upon the spiritual being he knew to be his timeless self. And so they did not understand that he could well have cured their bodies' ills, even had he not been, in the Spirit's world, the Luminary that he was.

Who could blame him if his mortal nature, weakened in a fateful hour, fell victim to an error, which made him trust the shouts of jubilant hosanna that offered him external might? Or that he would feel tempted by the thought of power, seemingly within his reach, even though he meant to use it only in the service of men's souls?

Here is where occurred that brief entanglement with guilt; a flaw not even this exalted life was able to escape; for none was ever born on earth who could remain untouched by sin.

Even though he purposefully sought to die by human hands, in the service of his highest spiritual mission—since only such a death enabled him to make the most sublime of gifts, which he alone was able to bestow—this death had come to face him much too soon. And so he needed all his inner strength to bear it willingly, and even pleaded with his *Father,* from the depth of his soul, to avert his earthly fate "if it were possible."

He still had "many things" to tell his pupils; things that, at the time, he clearly saw they were not yet prepared "to bear."

But when a messenger from the community of light of which he was a member came in the end to show him, in that agonizing vigil at Gethsemane, that even the *Father* of all those active in that radiant body could no longer alter the unfolding of events he had himself created, he once more found his inner powers, reclaimed his royal priesthood as a Luminary of Eternal Light and, as a hero, walked his final steps on earth, laden with the wooden yoke on which he was to perish.

Hanging on that malefactors' tree of torture, which then would give new meaning to a sacred symbol—revered by ancient venerable cults of ages long forgotten—he wrought his last and highest work of love: a mystery to all who in that hour stood about him, and even to this day a secret still to all except the rarest seers.

LET NO ONE THINK, however, that this death as such had been the substance of that final work of love.

The mystery accomplished here was an event I had reluctantly unveiled already in an earlier book; and also there I did so only in obedience to accepted duty.

May all those capable of comprehending comprehend it!

A fountainhead of spiritual energy has here been made accessible—to *every* human spirit on this planet—by the celestial might of love, of which this book would bring you word; a fountainhead of energy that could not be unlocked but by the sacrifice of one whose power of compassion was of boundless might.

The "God of vengeance," the most pernicious demon among the unseen fiends within the realms of the material cosmos, had here been vanquished—by a human mortal—through the *absolute elimination* of any sense of *hate* or *vengeance*. It was a task that could not be accomplished save by the Spirit's highest form of timeless love.

As for the rest of the events which, according to the ancient sources, supposedly occurred after the anointed Master's death, they are, historically considered, images of myth. It is a myth, however, that embodies truths of timeless depth.

The Master, thus, had truly "risen" from the dead. Yet in that "resurrection," he had no longer any use for his material body.

Again, the "young man in shining garment" was not by any means a vision merely of "affrighted" women. But also note the telling signs of truth, whose trace the writer of the ancient text could not erase; things he clearly neither recognized nor understood, but had to chronicle against his will, however much he then proceeded to obscure them.

To be sure, the Master's earthly body had not been taken from the tomb by his disciples; and so the writer of the ancient source could rightly claim that such reports were nothing more than rumors.

But in his days on earth the Master also had at times been meeting others; far from his disciples, in the solitude of the Judean mountains. Men who were not of his country, but peers of his own kind and, therefore, *one* with him in that community of Light in which he was a Brother, spiritually unified with all.

On one occasion he had chosen three among the Twelve to go with him into the mountains, where he used to "pray," and there permitted them to see his spiritual body's physical "transfiguration." Yet when these faithful souls beheld two figures next to him, garbed in "shining raiment," they thought these men were, surely, two among the ancient prophets —Moses and Elijah—so that the Master, deeply disappointed at their lack of understanding, charged them not to tell the others what they had observed.

He saw that, notwithstanding all his teaching, he could not wrest them from the bondage to their tribal faith, and that he merely would create confusion if he attempted to correct their error.

In fact, however, the "men in shining raiment" and the "youth" the women had encountered at the empty tomb were not strangers, unconnected with each other. And since they did not want to see their Brother's bodily remains become the object of a cult, they simply followed what in their country is the custom to this day in paying honor to a human being's temporal remains: they placed his body on a pyre, to let it be consumed by flames, after they had carefully prepared what needed to be done, at a selected site, well protected from intrusion.

Writing this I am informed by him who truly had authority to say that he would stay with mankind always, "until the end of the world." I am advised alike by the revered initiates, whom I may call my Brothers, who in that fateful night intentionally had caused the guards to fall into a deathlike sleep, that they themselves might carry out their Brother's will, which also was their own, with care and circumspection.

I know full well that many readers here will think me guilty of indulging self-delusions. Indeed, worse things than that will those who "blindly lead the blind" self-righteously suggest in order to dismiss my words.

One typically can recognize a crippled soul by its express denial of every revelation manifesting life it cannot apprehend, because it lacks the needed spiritual organs.

I am aware that here I touch on matters many look upon as sacrosanct. Even so, the teachings on salvation that love's most radiant Luminary brought the world are glorified more fittingly, indeed, by knowledge of the truth than by the vestiges of even the most ancient pious fraud, unknowingly committed and then routinely passed down through tradition. The latter ceases to be fraud, however, if one would but consider it *inspired poetry* that merely sought to veil historical events in garments of symbolic truth.

NOT EVEN THE MASS AWAKENING which then occurred at Jerusalem, at Pentecost, the Hebrew Feast of Weeks, was able to remove all clouds from every soul that now believed in the

Anointed, given that he had repeatedly been "seen" by his disciples following his death.

Too rigid were the chains that held these souls in bondage; and so the "Spirit of Truth," whom the Master once had promised, could not guide them to their own perfection.

St. Paul, the "Apostle of the Gentiles," the "teacher of the nations," was indeed a soul imbued with love, having once within himself *experienced* the "Spirit of Truth," his very being shaken to the core. From that day on he comprehended who the Master truly was; even so he met with bitter opposition when he faced those all too closely fettered minds who at that time could claim to be the pupils of the great Anointed.

But even he, the former pupil of the Pharisees, who then became the great proclaimer of the risen Christ, was not yet wholly free of misconceptions. And so he subsequently mingled, albeit in good faith, certain old traditional elements, familiar to him from his past, with the authentic teachings of the Master. Nonetheless, St. Paul saw matters far more clearly than did all those who called themselves "apostles" of a message that the

Master in his own words had announced as "joyful tidings."

Regrettably, the doctrine that was able, through the centuries, to spread its power over human souls, self-righteously appealing to the Master's having called it "joyful tidings," turned out to be decidedly *unjoyful.*

ST. JOHN, BY CONTRAST, the disciple whom the Master "loved," according to the ancient sources, removed himself and taught in secret; and those who sought the truth in silence remained attached to him.

He alone possessed the texts the Master once had, in his own hand, written and addressed to him. Only later did he give permission to a few whom he considered worthy to make copies of these writings for themselves.

Had Jesus truly, as is commonly assumed, taught through the spoken word alone, and not put anything in writing, one may rest assured that not one single word would have survived to our time the way he once had said it.

Both the manuscript's original and its copies were destroyed in later times, as I already stated in *The Wisdom of St. John,* by those who had preserved the Master's written words as their most venerated treasures, for fear these sacred texts might one day be profaned.

Of these matters, too, I only know through those who, in the realm of Spirit, are united with me, in Eternal Light, and who alone are capable of *knowing* these events. It is possible, however, that future generations may yet discover textual and other traces, which then will also physically confirm the truth of what I state. For, from the vantage point of spiritual perception, I am aware that parts of texts and fragments still exist on earth, although I am unable to identify the sites where they lie buried.

Certain traces, to be sure, are clearly visible to everyone in that part of the ancient gospel which tradition has in fact associated with the pupil whom the Master "loved."

The imperfections of this text are easily accounted for if one considers that its author, who was intimately allied with the circle of St. John's disciples, not only drew upon the writings by the Master's hand, but also wanted to combine them with other things he still possessed, in fragments, based upon tradition or on legends.

To be sure, nothing in the texts attributed to the disciple whom the Master "loved," was ever written by that pupil. Even so, the substance of the writings to which one gave his name is not too far removed from what he might have written, had he been the author.

YET ALL THESE QUESTIONS seem important only to a mind that would discover from *without* what ultimately can be comprehended only from *within*.

And it is also such who wonder where the great Anointed had been able to receive his wisdom; minds who then lend willing ears to sundry tales suggesting he had spent his "hidden years"—concerning which the gospel texts are silent—in India; while others claim that Egypt was the land where he had reached perfection.

There is no truth in either speculation.

Fact is that his earthly father had sought work in Egypt, where at the time the crafts were well rewarded, both to support his family and to return again with earnings he had saved—much as is the custom even nowadays of craftsmen coming from Italy and other lands—but at that time the one who later would embody timeless light was still a child and truly not mature enough to reach perfection of his mortal nature. Yet such perfection is the first condition each must have fulfilled who, in his mortal form, is consciously to apprehend his radiant individuation in Eternal Light.

To India, however, he surely had no need to journey; for what he needed from that land would make its way to him. And that majestic image of the "Wise Men from the East," the royal priests who had observed "his star," and came to offer him their gifts, had been connected with his early childhood only because the writers had themselves heard merely rumors touching this event. And there it also would be more effective in strengthening the wondrous aura they sought to link already with the Master's childhood

The fact that spiritual realities are comprehended only in one's spirit was obviously as foreign to the pious thinking of the ancient chroniclers as it seems even now to all who would today be moved by signs and wonders; despite the Master's admonition that only "in the Spirit" must one seek for God.

In the Master's childhood there was nothing in the least "miraculous"; indeed, necessity precluded any such occurrence.

He was a child like those who were his playmates; and when he had grown strong enough to help his father ply his strenuous trade, he learned the carpenter's profession like every member of that craft. In those days, however, a carpenter possessed the skill not only to build houses, but could also fashion a variety of other objects made of wood.

His *spiritual* unfolding, on the other hand, was kept in strictest secrecy, such as it is with each of like heredity within the Spirit. Yet what that spiritual development required did not in any way conflict with his external work.

NOR WAS THE MAN WHO, as a mortal human being, learned to comprehend his power in the Spirit—perfected long before his mother bore him his material body—resolved to stand aloof where earthly life would make demands; for had he been a stranger to this life on earth, he never would have reached his lofty goal.

He was a craftsman—until the hour tolled that claimed him for a different calling. And then he would give proof that he could "read the scriptures" better than the learned scribes, even though he had not studied "holy writ" as they had done.

As for the fakir tricks the chroniclers have heaped on him, he never did perform a single one. Yet certain "miracles" ascribed to him are symbols rich in meaning and, thus, profoundly true. His innate healing power, on the other hand, allowed him to accomplish deeds which his contemporaries saw as startling "miracles." But this particular gift had no connection whatsoever with his transcendent spiritual mission.

To suggest that he himself had ever used such "signs and wonders" as a basis for the claim that people *must believe* the things he taught, amounts to an outrageous defamation of a man who very clearly could distinguish between endowments of the flesh and powers of the Spirit. Only simple-minded lack of insight could have put those words into his mouth with which he seemed to be appealing to his "miracles"; but in this way the writers wanted to support the Master's teachings with scriptural, external proof.

The insights he revealed have been unscrupulously sinned against—for the sake of making "fishers of men." Indeed, the wrongs committed by the unenlightened missionaries of his hopelessly distorted teachings continue doing harm until this day; nor is the end of thus misleading seekers yet in sight.

May the following succeed in shedding light on certain crucial facts: for every reader who is yet inspired by *good will.*

The spiritual crisis of the many who lost faith in their beliefs, having known the Master's teachings only in corrupted form, and who continue to be led to further doubts by modern scholarly research that probes the ancient writings, has truly reached intolerable levels. At last, then, there is urgent need to find authentic answers that restore the truth.

Such, however, could not be expected save from those who know the author of these teachings as a living member of their circle. The very circle from which he had gone forth, sent by the *Father,* and to which he would return again the day his earthly mission was *accomplished.*

But from this source alone can one receive today, and in the future, the key to solving many an enigma. Also scholarship, directing its research from this perspective, shall in time be able to discover facts that can be ascertained, so that its explanations will even satisfy the minds of those who only "see" what they can "grasp."

All of searching mankind's questions that transcend the human being's merely physical existence as a mortal creature shall one day find their answer; after one has come to recognize, more and more distinctly, the active presence of the spiritual hierarchy, whose most significant and consequential messenger and agent was the Master of Nazareth.

HOW WRONGLY ARE ALL THOSE advised who seem to think the teachings of this Luminary merely sought to recommend the feeble sentiment that commonly one praises as the "love for all mankind"!

Often their advisers found it difficult to give the Master's actions, as they are recorded in the Gospels, the suitable interpretation that was necessary, in their judgment, to buttress their beliefs.

There are matters, to be sure, that somehow will not fit the image if one attempts to foist the saccharine weakling, "meek and mild," whom pious pulpit oratory fashioned, upon the portrait of the records.

The forceful personality these writings still preserve, notwithstanding their corruption, bears scant resemblance to the images of fulsome sweetness that enfeebled faith invented as a reflection of its own anemic life.

Many a word in "holy writ" can be adjusted to support these images only if a conscience void of due restraint will misconstrue that word, so that its explanation will provide the sense required; until the last authentic fragments shall be lost that have escaped the damage done in early days.

That kind of treacly exegete of holy writ would surely deem it blasphemous to think the radiant Master could have, in his earthly life, himself experienced the very love his "servant" clearly senses in his flesh and blood —permitted to him by his creed, or no—but which he must reject as "sinful," being ignorant of its divine connectedness.

Blasphemous would in his judgment be the very thought that this corporeal form of love might draw its essence from the same eternal source whose radiance also flows through love's celestial revelation, manifested in the venerated Master's life in word and deed; that highest form of all, wherein he found the strength to bring about the cosmic deed of love through which he consecrated, from the gibbet of the Roman cross, all of mankind by the power of his royal priesthood in the Spirit.

And yet, my friend, you shall not ever find the love the Master knew if you awaken only maudlin sentiments within yourself and call your sympathy for mankind, merged with pity, by the name of "love."

This feeble likeness of imagined "love" is hard to reconcile with the portrayal of the

Master who, burning with contempt for the contemptible, made himself a "scourge of cords," in his disciples' midst, to drive the public merchants from the temple they defiled; the man who overturned the money changers' tables with a kick, and made the priesthood of his people hear the scathing accusations which their vengeful minds could never afterwards forgive.

To make such deeds accord with one's own lack of inner calling, it was found necessary to invent the concept of the Master's "godlike wrath." And thus one felt no scruples in ascribing to the Master's *Father in Heaven* all those vindictive traits which ancient, fear-evoking priestly lore had made the emblem of a dire tribal god. An idol that the great Anointed once had spiritually toppled from its throne when he pronounced the mighty word: "But I say unto you . . ."

No, my friend! If you would truly see eternal love beget reality and life within you, the paths you must pursue are very different from those your teachers used to show you.

Can you not comprehend that love upon its highest level will not reveal its power in a weaker form than where its presence, even on a lower rung, already heightens all your senses, actions, and pursuits, so that you often shatter barriers you once had thought unbreakable?

Only if you seek an energy within you that awakens, even at the highest spiritual level, the selfsame inner powers, and will master all things else that hold you still in bondage, shall you find within yourself the kind of love that was embodied in the Master's life.

Not until that day shall you attain the freedom promised to the "children of light," and find the "peace that this world cannot give."

AGAIN, YOU MUST NOT THINK the words the ancient records have preserved are meant to give you new "commandments."

Trust me, and do not let your understanding be deceived by texts that long ago had been corrupted: Never did the Master use the word "commandment," nor did he give the like at any time.

Not even the "commandment" to his pupils to "love one another" did he ever utter in the form in which it is recorded.

At most he would at times cite "scripture"—"Thou shalt love thy neighbor as thyself"—to let the orthodox fanatics of his people know that also he was well acquainted with their "law."

The fact his pupils were accustomed to be "given" and to "keep commandments," was the reason that his counsels were transformed into commands. The only way his followers could understand his admonitions was by turning them into "commandments."

Faithfully observing ancient Jewish practice, they needed both: commandments—and the threat of punishment, if such injunctions were not kept.

Thus, when the Master spoke on how *salvation* is attained, they freely used his words to formulate a sort of recipe that would secure *salvation*. For, in their narrow understanding one needed no more than to keep "commandments," to be assured of being *saved* within the world to come.

In this respect they acted much like the beclouded minds today who like to think that inner light and clarity of apprehension may be gained by means of sundry mystifying "exercises," which continue to be hailed, again and again, in rather dubious publications.

YET EVEN THE AUTHENTIC parts the ancient source contained were in reality, already in its very first redaction, no more than fading echoes of the Master's teachings. At best these parts were based on recollections of events that, at the time of writing, had occurred whole decades in the past.

It is nothing short of blasphemy to hold the Spirit of Eternity accountable for texts whose authors—already captured by the spell of ancient phantom gods whose cults proliferated in their days in novel guise, and still a long way from rejecting blind submission to a vengeful tribal god—attempted to preserve the Master's vaguely recollected teachings, newly formed according to their own still hazy understanding, so that they were unable even to suspect the scope of their distortions.

Never did the radiant Master give "commandments" to his pupils; or else he had not been the sovereign Luminary that he was, still is, and shall eternally remain.

The form in which he gave his teachings was: "Blessed are you!" and "Woe unto you!"—such as are the teachings of all his spiritual Brothers, of all who, in the Spirit's realm, are one with him as fellow workers for mankind.

He offered blessings and he uttered condemnations, but never did he use the word "commandment" when he taught.

As a Luminary, a Mediator of Eternal Light, he knew full well that mere observance of "commandments" will never gain one blessings, and that *salvation* cannot be attained if one does not desire it *unbidden*—freely, by an act of will.

If, then, you hope to salvage the Master's genuine teachings from the ancient texts, you will admittedly have to discard a great deal you had grown to love from childhood on. Certain parts again you will be able to retain and carefully preserve, precisely since you recognized them as additions made by other hands.

Be careful, lest you should reject too much of what you deem in error.

The one thing you ought not to do is trust in modern rationalistic speculation as the touchstone of your judgment.

Practice patience for a while, until the true and deeper meaning of my words awakens confirmation in your own discernment.

I gave you the criteria you need if you would recognize the still authentic "sayings of the Lord."

But, in addition, also bear in mind the following:

"Kyrios," meaning "Sir," is even nowadays the form one uses to address, wherever Greek is spoken, any man who is not patently a beggar.

"Kyrie eleyson" is the beggar's plea when, sitting by the roadside, he lifts his eyes in supplication to move the passers-by to pity.

Bearing this in mind will keep you from ascribing, out of false respect, a meaning to the title "Lord," occurring in the ancient sources, which this word at that time did not have, and would not gain until much later, long after the Master's death, in the usage of the newly forming cult.

His pupils called him *Rabbi,* and also this address may lead to misinterpretation; given that today this is the public title of only the ordained official leader of a Jewish congregation.

Even nowadays, however, a learned scholar of the scriptures in a Jewish community may be honored by the title *rabbi,* notwithstanding that in daily life he may pursue a secular profession.

And only in that way was it bestowed upon the Galilean carpenter who could "reveal the scriptures" to his followers, because he was a Master in the Spirit's light; a member of that radiant spiritual body that is active here on earth. You may have heard that fellowship referred to as the "Great White Brotherhood," or as the "White Lodge"; names that are of recent date, which I use merely since their imagery is suitable.

Those who are his peers and Brothers—inseparably *one* with him in spiritual union, as he himself is *one* with them—revere him as the greatest of Compassion's Mediators. For none before him had accomplished that transcending work of timeless love to which he, of his own free will, had made himself a sacrifice. And after him no other can perform a deed that one might even distantly compare to his surpassing work of love. By virtue of his sacrifice the *spiritual aura* of this earth has been transformed, for all the ages yet to come, and for each human mortal. Owing to this transformation, every human being now is able to gain access to dimensions of the Spirit's realm which very few had had the strength to reach before, and only after agonizing struggles of overcoming their own selves.

I KNOW FULL WELL I CANNOT by mere words reveal to you the nature of the love whose life was manifested in the greatest Mediator of Compassion ever to have lived on earth.

I can only show you how you may detect authentic traces of that life, despite the layers of debris that cover the reports whose writers sought to tell you of his teachings.

May you sense the message of that life in all its purity within your heart of hearts, wherein alone it is received in its true power, so that the Master find in you a worthy pupil!

Yet bear in mind that everything I am allowed to give you also issues from the same eternal source Yehoshuah had drawn upon in his own day, given that he was a Mediator of Eternal Light.

Nor is there any word the radiant Mediator of Compassion ever said about his person which I could not say also of myself , and in the same way that he meant it, if there were any need.

In one respect alone I, too, must bow to him in veneration. But knowing what that one exception is, I also know that there is none among my spiritual Brothers who does not equally, in this respect, look up to him in awe.

What sets him thus apart, however, is the boundless might of love that in himself and through his work had found its living manifest expression.

His love will also be the source from which your own life shall arise, if you are able to discern what I would make you comprehend in all my writings.

Regard yourself as blessed if you "take no offense in me," although the man of whom I speak perhaps became a "God" in your imagination also; much as he has in the belief, self-induced or taught by others, of countless human minds, despite the fact that in his days on earth he would have found the harshest words not harsh enough to castigate such godlike veneration of his person.

But here I am not speaking of the "God" whom the opinions of innumerable intellects have lifted up within these last two thousand years. The "God" to whom they gave the name and image of Compassion's greatest Mediator, as their teachers, lacking vision and impelled by fear, insisted that they should.

I speak, instead, of only the historic human mortal whose temporal and timeless life had been united with the Spirit's realm; the same who, following his earthly body's torture, agony, and death, had then become, but quite against his will, the chosen model of a God whose image bears the all too human limitations of its makers.

The longing that inspires human beings to fashion gods for worship in the image of their kind reveals a need whose deepest roots I know. And, like yourself, I also truly honor the exalted forms of human life that, shaped by fervent faith, according to their makers' mortal lights, then served the world through centuries as objects of religious veneration.

However, I am at the same time unified inseparably with the spiritual individuation whose historical appearance had become the unintended cause that such an image of external worship could later be erected in his name.

To serve as voice and witness of that eternal individuation has been made my duty by the spiritual structure of eternal life, which brought my being forth, out of itself, even as it once had born that Master's individuation, embodied in a mortal human form.

The time will come when these disclosures will not be looked upon as either blasphemous presumption, nor as a sign suggesting a beclouded mind.

CHAPTER TWO

ON LOVE'S PRIMORDIAL FIRE

Do not profess you know of love as long as cares about yourself still weigh upon your mind.

Even as the "lilies in the field," which in the East grow wild across the land, and like "the fowls of the air," you must no more "take thought" and fret about yourself if you would come to know love's highest form within you.

As long as you are still consumed by common, fear-inspired worry about yourself and your existence here on earth—a fear that plainly shows your lack of trust in life that is eternal—you truly do not know about the kind of love the radiant Master taught; the love through which alone your spirit shall gain freedom.

You make yourself your worry's slave and yet, with all your anguish you accomplish nothing.

And all the while, the most divine of energies lies dormant in your being, because you do not know how to employ its power.

PERHAPS YOU "love wholeheartedly" all those you feel are "dear" to you and whom you would not ever want to lose in life on earth. And possibly you even made yourself embrace a universal "love of all humanity." Indeed, you say, your "love" embraces even animals, and plants, and every sight your eyes behold?

It may surprise you, then, to hear me tell you that even so your life is hardly yet imbued with love's celestial power.

Your native tongue can here become your teacher; for when you say you "love" a certain person—in your conception of that word—you simply state that you are fond of having those you "love" about you.

What is important to you in your "love" is the idea of "having"—of possessing what you love—together with the pleasure granted by such "having"; even if it merely were possession gained through seeing, hearing, or the knowledge that a fellow human being, living with you or perhaps in distant parts, emotionally belongs to you in life.

The love, by contrast, that Compassion's greatest Mediator spoke of in his teachings, the love of which I tell you in the present book, is a primordial *spiritual* energy, yet at the same time closely interwoven also with all *earthly* life. This power must pervade your being, even as the lower form of that same energy will overwhelm you with its all-consuming fire when you feel the flames of earthly passion burning in your soul.

When you experience *earthly* love, you still desire to possess; for here your love would grasp and hold the object of its passion. In its *celestial* form, however, love becomes the object that is longing for *itself*, and here all feelings of desire will have left you.

In *earthly* love you are forever reaching out for some external thing you long to get your hands on and draw towards you. In its *celestial* form, by contrast, love becomes an inner radiance, a fire spreading light and warmth —a boundless overflowing from within that comprehends all things that lie without.

ONLY THAT CELESTIAL FORM of love brings forth all real miracles of spiritual awakening; and it alone will cause all that to come about as *of itself* which you today still try to gain by outward effort, expecting that some magic method or mysterious exercise might one day bring you what you seek.

Needless to say, your friendly feelings for humanity and your emotional possessiveness, which you regard as "love," can never let you gain the power that, in the expression's truest sense, is "mightier than death."

But everything that until now you were accustomed to consider "love"—when not referring to mere physical desire—will truly find its full perfection when you yourself shall be imbued with love's primordial fire.

From the depth of your entire being then shall flow in rich abundance what today you still endeavor to accomplish with much toil.

What you today still feel to be your "duty," or may regard a deed of "virtue," will then be simply the most natural and obvious fulfillment of your daily life.

Nor can you cause the flames of love's primordial fire to consume your soul without its rays continuously flowing from your depth, and all that shall come near you will sense that constant radiance.

Everything you had before encountered as aggression or resistance shall then desire, of its own accord, to join and to ally itself with your own self and will.

Your very life must undergo an inner change, however, if you would see yourself transformed into a sun enflamed by love's celestial fire.

Without this conscious will to change, without consistently maintaining this new orientation of your life, you are not likely to experience highest love.

You must be *willing* to transform yourself, if you would truly see your very self transformed.

UNTIL THIS DAY YOU WERE like someone asking to be given—even in the Spirit's world—what he desires to possess. But here you can be given only what is not already yours; without regard to what you are requesting, and whether you may know of what you own, or not.

Now the celestial form of love I here describe is a capacity that you already own, albeit unawares; and so you need no more be given what you in fact possess. You alone, however, must decide to use this spiritual capacity in order that it may reveal its nature in you.

You must desire to become a *sun*—a *sun* that wills to shine of its own self—and once you shall continuously foster that resolve, the fire of love's highest self-expression will more and more resplendently reveal its light within you.

You still are too afraid to be consumed by this eternal fire.

The foolish fear that you could somehow *lose* yourself prevents your will from daring what you ought to dare.

You well may feel a kind of modest warmth within yourself; you call this feeling "love" and, quite content, desire nothing more. But then you seem surprised and wonder why the feeble radiance this "love" emits remains without effect within you and without; indeed, proves wholly powerless to mold your fate on earth.

You do not know the strength of radiant energy you might in fact attain if you yourself were willing to become a *sun,* instead of passively expecting to be warmed and nourished merely by the spiritual rays of other *suns.*

Everything within yourself must henceforth be resolved to *give,* if—out of your own self—you would *receive* the highest gift you own within.

While you may judge what at this stage you have to offer but a wretched pittance, even so, this humble tribute will be quite sufficient to kindle your potential radiance, provided that your will remains resolved to give to others more than to expect from them.

THERE IS A STORY of an Indian prince who one day asked a yogi to describe the feelings of a sage who has attained perfection. To this the yogi replied that once he likewise had been asked about the feelings of a lover, but that the only answer he had then been able to give was the advice, "You shall know that—once you are in love."

In the same way, also I can only speak in images about the highest form of love as an eternal cosmic power; for I could no more properly explain to you this *heavenly* reality of love than I am able to impart through words a semblance of the feeling one calls *earthly* love, given that it manifests itself exclusively in life on earth.

In either case you must allow love's fire to consume your being if you would truly comprehend its power, both in its physically determined, and in its highest spiritual form.

As a mortal human being you are by nature able to feel *earthly* love, and this capacity resides in you even during times when passion does not stir your soul. In the same way, however, there is within you at all times, albeit still unknown to you, also the *celestial* form of that same power, whose effects reach far beyond this mortal life, endowing you with all but godlike freedom here on earth; for everything you may encounter is subject to its might.

It was of this celestial form of love and of its spiritual omnipotence the Master of Nazareth had spoken and borne witness, and he himself drew all his power from that source.

It also was this kind of love that had awakened in the one who then became the greatest missionary of the Master's teachings when, speaking of himself, he said, "And if I had not love, I would be no more than a sounding brass and a tinkling cymbal." Both will give off sounds if struck by something from without, but lack the inner life that could create its own sound from within.

The love, by contrast, that we here discuss proceeds at all times from its own accord within, independent of external causes.

How much longer yet shall human hearts on earth exclude themselves from being guided by such love?

Very few have known of its existence—few have made themselves its vessel—of all the generations that throughout the centuries have lived to see the sunlight here on earth.

The forces of external nature have long since yielded to mortal man's dominion and control. Within their inner world, by contrast, human beings seem content with making merely feeble efforts to compromise with their inherent energies, because they are not conscious of the timeless power that would not merely make them masters of the energies within their physical existence, but also capable of thoroughly affecting their external world; if only a substantial part of mankind were prepared to unify its will within that inner power.

Wherever human souls have found their way from darkness into light; wherever greatness was revealed in deeds whose light shone through the centuries; wherever in a human's life the instincts of the mortal creature were conquered by the Spirit's light—in each such case that power had awakened in the heart of *one* and then was able to inspire and awaken *many.*

Again and again, however, those in whom this fire had been kindled allowed its godly flames to die, because they had grown weary of nourishing its radiance by drawing on their own resources.

Nor is there hope to end these present days of gloom and mindless hate, which once again have granted power to the "God of vengeance," whose tyranny the teachings of Compassion's greatest Mediator long since had enabled mankind to defeat; these days when human minds in Babel-like confusion pervert the impulse of creative will into a poisoned madness of destruction; these days, which fall upon a wretched generation like hammer blows by legions of demented fiends that would reduce to rubbish heaps amidst barbarian chaos every monument the Spirit's light had ever raised in triumph over brutish sloth—nor is there hope to bring these dark days to an end until that end shall be accomplished by the power of celestial love.

The smoldering wall of flames whose sooty clouds today send noxious fumes across the planet's lands and seas will not be quenched by cataracts of breezy slogans that orators dispense with sweeping gestures.

The sprouting green that now must perish in this blaze had longed for sunlight and for warmth, but as it found no *sun* these days to guide its growth, its search for light and warmth misled it to fall prey to fires from a nether realm.

Blessed are those who need not to themselves confess, "I, too, must be included among the voices by whom the forest of young trees that here is devastated in a world-wide sea of flames had felt its longing for the sunlight's warmth betrayed."

In vain are now all efforts to extinguish flames that must exhaust themselves before at last they die. Still, one should not be deceived; the hearts of those who did not perish in this blaze continue longing after light and warmth as much as ever, because this impulse was awakened by a cosmic will; nor is there any might on earth that could prevent its spiritual fulfillment.

But to fulfill that longing, there is need for radiant human *suns* who never tire sharing light and inner warmth.

Such inherent longing will be gifted with discernment, and thus it shall reject all things that lack the radiance imparted by the Spirit's love.

What now has been reduced to smoldering ashes is doubtless lost forever and therewith priceless treasures mankind once possessed. The newly sprouting seedlings of the earth shall not, however, be destroyed a second time, nor once again become the tempting prey that netherworldly flames are craving to devour.

Here, too, the Spirit's highest helpers truly offer their protection; even though they had not been allowed to hold back from destruction what in itself contained the will to be destroyed, albeit without knowing.

The guardians of the Spirit that are here at work shall carefully protect each newly risen sprout and keep it shielded from consuming flames. As mankind's truest friends, and counselors of deepest understanding, they also shall not brook the rattling skeletons that flap like monstrous bats in capes of countless folds before the sun, but, moved with pity, send them back into their tombs, so that the Spirit's primal sun at last can pour the light and warmth of all its rays on every soul alive on earth.

It is from this primordial *sun* alone that all the radiant energy proceeds which manifests itself within the individuated spiritual *suns*, whose presence mankind on this planet needs, even as the countless hosts of planets that range throughout the universe depend upon their multitudes of fiery stars to keep their orbits in harmonious paths.

THE THRESHOLD AT WHICH mankind stands today is not, as some imagine the "decline" of Western culture. Instead, it is that culture's highest future rise that now exacts the sacrifices all discerning human beings of the West have every reason to lament.

"Whoever has ears to hear with, let him hear!"

The portents of the age must truly not be read the way that ruminating skeptics fancy, who seek the multitude's applause by deftly juggling thoughts, as acrobats will dazzle crowds with balls.

What this present age has need of is, instead, "the faith and patience of the saints."

Not such as fancy they are "holy," because like creeping worms they slither out of all accountability and guilt, but those discerning mortals who apprehend the presence of salvation and thus became, as some have done in every age, "the salt of the earth."

Already our children's children will no longer know these days of crazed delusions, which now are drawing to a close, even though their final end may still appear quite distant.

That generation will no longer even comprehend the pathological derangement of the minds who at this time provide the stage for insane capers, given that, ensnared by gloomy powers, whose thralls they willingly became, they opened wide the doors to rampant folly. And so they view the "human being" merely as the wretched mortal animal—more pitiful, indeed, than any other creature on this planet—which man on earth must judge himself to be as long as he has not yet recognized that in his mortal earthly form he is in truth the timeless human spirit's portal to salvation.

Yet only this awareness will bring the human self the fully conscious certainty that love's celestial form alone can offer it the unimagined power so thoroughly to change this planet's face that all the misery which humans find on earth: that sickness, suffering, and want must vanish from their lives; even as the fearsome beasts have disappeared which *early man*—the animal in its emerging human form—at first had fled, but later learned to vanquish.

All of us who in these days of darkness feel death's oppressive shadow weigh upon our souls are burying a bygone age; yet, at the same time, we are bringing forth the coming life that one day shall inspirit this external earth.

It is from us that all the generations which this planet still is meant to shelter shall on that day demand account when finally the cosmic

"It is finished!"

will resound throughout the myriad spheres where human spirits had sought refuge after they had willfully detached themselves from life in God and thus, like precious driftwood, were cast upon the currents of an unknown fate.

It is what we pursue today that either shall transform this planet's face, or must obstruct this transformation, even though it will be future generations who will reap the harvest—according to the seeds that we put in the ground.

YET DO NOT THINK that we might not ourselves already see our work fulfilled, even though we may be granted merely blossoms where future generations will harvest ample crops.

The sooner we shall rouse ourselves to act as spiritually awakened beings, the sooner also shall our actions, which our hearts perform, reward us with the sight of the unfolding blossoms that others, living after our time, shall one day find as ripened fruit.

To our will has fate bequeathed a treasure of immeasurable worth in these profoundly earnest days. And, thus, one truly may exclaim, *It is a joy to be alive"** at such a time as this, for all who, fully conscious of their own responsibility, have recognized the value of their own existence for the future of all coming generations.

WHERE ARE THEY NOW, the foolish dreamers who in their day believed the phantoms of their minds would prove immortal?

Forgotten like the lowest among beggars, whose name no chronicle records, their labors vanish in a coming age whose dawn they could not fathom nor anticipate because, intoxicated with their wealth of knowledge, they felt convinced their intellect's unfailing light would brightly shine for all the generations yet to come.

*"*Juvat vivere*" is the famous phrase Ulrich von Hutten (1488-1523) coined in a letter to Willibald Pirckheimer (1470-1530) on December 25, 1515.

And even now there are among us vain pretenders who regard themselves as sages and find their satisfaction in posing as initiates.

Not all may be aware that they deceive, and some indeed believe they serve the truth. Nonetheless, this age of radical devaluation of all values has also spawned a host of minds who feel no longer bound by any trace of conscience once they are themselves possessed by their delusions. And so they will lead thousands to destruction through their teachings, spellbound by their power to bewilder human souls, and by conceit beclouded when they see the columns of believers who march behind their banners.

"For false Christs and false prophets shall rise . . ."

Be mindful of such signs, which mark the present age, and do not let yourselves be caught in fiendish nets from whose entanglements not many can escape.

AS YOU WOULD NOT ENTRUST a charlatan and his elixirs with your mortal body's life when its survival is at stake, so should you likewise never put your soul into the hands of anyone who tells you that he knows how to preserve your soul's eternal life.

Although there may be few things in this life concerning which you feel unquestionably certain, you surely will possess a certainty of instinct alerting you to danger when the survival of your suffering mortal body is at risk.

The same unfailing certainty is yours, however, when your soul's well-being is in danger; but since you can destroy and lose your soul without imperiling your mortal body's life, you no longer heed the inner warnings you are given when the life of your eternal soul is threatened.

Yet even as suspicion instantly will rise in you, if you have but the slightest judgment, when in your body's physical distress a charlatan approaches you, so shall you likewise sense an inner warning when in the anguish of your soul a teacher offers you his guidance who well may be in greater need of guidance than yourself, and whom you merely called because you did not know of any other help.

Still, you are not for that reason free of guilt if you entrust yourself to teachers who mislead;

because eternal nature endowed your feeling with the power of discernment; and thus it simply is your own indifference if you do not at once perceive that you are blindly following a "spiritual guidance" that is itself in dire need of being led.

Living in these earnest days you must be doubly cautious, since now you have been made aware, by what I had to tell you, that countless future generations shall be greatly furthered—or impeded—by your present actions.

It is the innate will of love's primordial fire to shine in you as *life*, in order that this fire's *life*, continuing to shine through you, may then bring forth new *life* in turn—here, within the hearts of mortals who on earth are laboring to give their being its eternal form.

But if your own life was not born of love, how would you then become the source that will create new life?

That is why I here was bound to show you, to the extent one can by means of words, what the transcendent energy of love encompasses in truth. The very love to which an ancient source bears witness, documenting lives in whom its godlike form was manifest.

That is also why I had to let you see the truth about the life and teachings of the greatest Mediator of that love who once had wrought compassion's most exalted work.

In his embodiment of love's sublime perfection he triumphantly released the rigid fetter that had enclosed all human life on earth in its relentless iron grip, ever since the first of human spirits had sought shelter on this planet in the forms of mortal creature life.

But what he taught was also this, "If anyone would be my pupil, let him follow me."

Ludicrously foolish are the dreamers who assume they merely need to mimic, in external mannerisms, the supposed gestures of this most powerful of spiritual sovereigns to see themselves acknowledged by him as "disciples"; or, more accurately, in the language of the records, as his *pupils*.

If they had but the faintest notion of who he truly was—and is—they surely would swear off their folly.

But you, the reader whom I here address, should not like them become the servile captive of such gross delusions.

By now you surely are sufficiently instructed and informed.

If you truly are resolved to prove yourself a worthy pupil of the Galilean carpenter, who was a Luminary of primordial Light, as is the writer of the present book, then be determined to awaken in yourself the highest form of love, whose fire must consume your being before its power can endow you with new life.

Only then have you in truth become his pupil, his disciple.

Only then will he acknowledge you as one in whom his love has come to life, even as he knew his own life rooted in his *Father's* love.

Then only will he recognize and know you as one of those the *Father* loves, because they gained perfection in the *Father's Son.*

Then only shall Yehoshuah, the carpenter of Nazareth, of whom the ancient writings bring you word, but who became estranged from you by minds in bondage to the myths of early pagan gods; minds who deemed him all too close to human nature, so that they draped him in the phantom vestments of their idols —then only shall you feel him coming near you so that you can in truth proclaim:

"I know that my Redeemer liveth!"—the *Son of Man,* who in his day could rightfully assure his pupils that he would spiritually abide with them, "unto the end of the world."

ONLY LOVE'S PRIMORDIAL power can make one capable of truly keeping such a pledge.

For one who has attained perfection in the Spirit's world it unavoidably becomes a sacrifice of indescribable severity, continuously offered, in having to sustain his timeless self, after the material body's death, in a condition wherein he will remain accessible to human feelings in their physically constricted mortal state.

But one should not imagine that this self-imposed abiding in the field of spiritual energy that mortal human consciousness is able to attain—a state that I and all who are my kindred in the Spirit know in all its forms—

involves some kind of mystery-enshrouded "miracle."

Objectively considered, it is nothing other than a *focused stabilizing* of a Mediator's consciousness, in strict conformity with spiritual law; a state that will outlast the functional resources of the mortal human body by immeasurable ages—to the distant time when finally the last vibrations of spiritual seeking shall have ceased within the aura of this planet.

How very great a sacrifice must here be made reveals itself already in the fact that one is obligated, by necessity, to stay connected to a self-created body—which mortal senses are not able to perceive, although it still forms part of the unseen dimension of the world of matter—and to confine one's timeless consciousness within the limitations of that body for eternities.

At the same time, however, such a *focused stabilizing* of his consciousness imposes the necessity upon the Mediator to experience, as his own, the suffering of human souls throughout mankind. Only the primordial fire of celestial love can grant a Luminary the resources to endure this state of sharing all of human grief within his self-restricted consciousness until the last among his human fellow souls has finally returned into the world of light.

CHAPTER THREE

LIGHT OF LIBERATION

Those who read these words in our time have grown up with the teachings of the most diverse religious faiths and it is difficult to guide their hearts toward that sublime all creeds transcending single source from which salvation's liberating rays of love eternally descend into the world of human souls, where they set free what had been bound, and then return again into the timeless wellspring of all love, whose depth imparts the love that forms its very being.

There well may be self-righteously convinced "believers" who with a haughty smile look down on what I say, feeling safe in their hypnotic mental self-appeasement, never doubting that their lemming creed alone must be the "sole true faith."

Others, who long since have rejected all religious bondage may have to overcome ingrained suspicion if they assume the teachings I convey are merely resurrected echoes of mankind's oldest speculations, now newly draped in modern guise. Indeed, were this the case, such only would cast human souls into still deeper darkness.

Yet what I offer here will give to either group no less than the most solid grounds on which to base their own convictions; because a faith that fails to reach its teachings' deepest roots lacks all foundation; and knowledge of whatever kind will rest on solid footing only if its facts are anchored on the bedrock of eternity.

It is the liberating light of timeless love which here my words would kindle in your soul; be it that you still embrace a life of pious faith according to revered tradition, or rather live according to your own beliefs and rules.

And when I here bear witness to Compassion's greatest Mediator—whom a rigidly dogmatic creed imagines to have *risen* solely for its own believers, despite the fact they all too often used his image as a shield to hide the hatred in their deeds—my witness is in truth the work of his own will. For in that final sacrifice of love, which he accomplished in his dying hour, he consecrated *all of humankind.* He thus became—for every human spirit—the *savior* and *redeemer* from a bondage that could be broken only by a Mediator of celestial love whose powers to unfold the fires of that cosmic force surpassed all others who on earth were vessels of that highest form of love.

He that, in the full perfection of his radiant glory, once had given his own self to all mankind, after having first intended to bring spiritual fulfillment only to the nation in whose midst he had been born, is close to all that call on him. And everyone can find him who will seek him in his love. Nor does it matter whether you observe traditional forms of worship—which have preserved much ancient wisdom that you indeed may honor once your spirit makes you see their truth—or whether you regard these forms as alien to your nature and call upon him purely from your heart of hearts in ways and words that are your own.

Unified with those in whose domain of light he had been one before his birth into a mortal body here on earth, he is alive today within this planet's spiritual dimension; present in a timeless form of absolute reality, which had become his own when he returned his soul into his *Father's* hands.

AS I ALREADY TOLD YOU in another book, to the extent one can by means of words, the *Father* of all Luminaries of eternal Light embodies the primordial light-begotten Human Being of the Spirit, eternally engendered by the *Word of the Beginning*; the One who is Himself the *Word* within the *Word*, and *God with God*; the Ancient of Days abiding in the Origin; the One who is Himself the firstborn self-creation of the *Word*; the *Human of Eternity*, present through the aeons in his first, primordial generation.

Ancient teachings venerate that Being as the highest among "angels," as the "crown" of the eternal hierarchy of spirits who themselves created, here on earth, the Luminaries of eternal Light, to be the *builders* of the cosmic *bridge* that will guide human mortals from the realm of animal existence, allowing them to find and to return again to their immortal spirits' home, from which they willfully had torn themselves eternities ago.

In each such Luminary of primordial Light this *Father* is eternally begetting his own *Son,* the individuated Luminary. The *Father's* essence, thus, is truly, in the full sense, of *one single nature* with that Luminary's timeless self. Yet for the latter's individuation, this earth's material body serves merely as a tool whereby the Mediator can effect, within the earthly realm, what must appear in earthly form if human mortals are to apprehend it.

And, thus, the Master of Nazareth clearly spoke the truth when he declared, "He that has seen me has seen the Father"; and, "No one comes to the Father, but by me"—through that which has been given life in *me,* who is the *Father's Son,* eternally begotten in the Spirit.

Helpers willing to assist you have thus been born into this mortal life on your behalf, close at all times to your spirit if you are able *spiritually* to call them—by your deeds.

"Not everyone who says to me 'Lord, Lord,' shall enter into the kingdom of heaven, but he that does the will of my Father"—one who feels that will within his soul and then fulfills it through his works.

Yet wishful thinking will avail you nothing. You need to "call" by means of your entire conduct in this life, by all your actions and pursuits. And not a few unnoticed, humble souls who faithfully attended merely to their daily work had "called" for spiritual guidance more effectively than many a celebrity who mastered all the sacred scriptures and long had felt that meeting inner guidance was his due, so that his dignity be elevated even further, in both his own and in the public's estimation.

HUMAN INGENUITY WAS able to design the telescope; an instrument containing a variety of hidden lenses and reflectors, which in their apt arrangement will effect that even the most distant objects seem quite near and can be recognized as three-dimensional bodies.

When using such a telescope you obviously will have to look through only the specific lens the maker of the instrument intended for that purpose.

Your eye will then receive the rays of light that are reflected in this world of matter in such a way that distant objects are brought close to your perception, so that you can distinguish details which your naked eye would never have discerned.

And likewise are you able, in the Spirit's world, to apprehend the light of Godhead only if at first you turn to those whom the primordial Light of the Beginning has itself prepared to be its Mediators, in order that they may convey its rays to you in earthly form.

You then shall—through that Luminary—only apprehend the Godhead's light as such, while he himself shall disappear; even as, when looking through a telescope, you do not see the individual lenses, but rather the specific object of your search.

But just as, in the telescope, the single lens within the eyepiece would not be of much use unless the instrument included, in addition, a series of connected lenses and reflectors, so the Luminary likewise could not offer you his help unless the Spirit's timeless hierarchy existed as a bridge between himself and God's primordial reality, which is the goal to be attained.

When a Luminary of primordial Light reveals himself to you, out of his spiritual nature, your eye is looking, as it were, through all dimensions of this spiritual hierarchy, directly into the profoundest depth of God.

This image lets you form a truer understanding of many a word the Master of Nazareth had spoken to his pupils. You thus will learn to differentiate between the things he spoke on his behalf, as a mortal human of his time and place, and those exalted sayings, pronounced at moments when he himself would vanish, to make you only hear the Godhead's inmost voice, the timeless Word of the Beginning. For, clearly, what applies to seeing in the image used above, you easily can also understand in terms of hearing.

A DIFFERENT ANALOGY WILL let you better comprehend another truth.

Even as a fountain displaying many spouts will nonetheless from each discharge the selfsame water, flowing from their common source —each lending to that water jet a different form, according to its own unique design— so, too, each member of the Brotherhood of

Light for which I speak will always teach you but the same objective truth; even though, in its external garb, that truth may seem to differ, owing to the teacher's individuality.

You firmly need to bear this fact in mind if you would learn to recognize, even in the most diverse external garments, invariably the one eternally unalterable truth, which may appear in any form its Mediator chooses, yet will in essence always be the same.

And likewise you receive, in all the insights I am granted to express in words, nothing other than the light that had imbued the teachings of Yehoshuah, Compassion's greatest Mediator. Thus, you here may see a different form of teaching, yet one that also draws its waters from the same eternal well.

Indeed, you only will begin correctly to interpret that radiant Master's mighty word, which even now still shines through layers of debris, when you have come to know my writings. And what I state you will not fully comprehend in its true depth until you recognize his timeless nature, as clearly as you must, if you would not have ancient fables so distort his image in your mind that very little still reflects the living person that he *was—and has remained until this very day.*

For someone in my situation, who in this day and age is obligated to unlock the way to truth and shed new light on facts that darkness had enshrouded for millennia, this obligation truly is a heavy burden A still more painful yoke, however, do I find the need to forego all protective outer garments and utterly to bare my spiritual life and nature to the leering vulture stares that cannot be averted wherever truth reveals herself on earth, before eternal love has made all human souls shine brightly in its flames.

The obligation here fulfilled has truly been a painful, bitter cup; nor can anyone appreciate the struggles in which my inmost self was forced to war against the mortal being, whose life I live in this external world, before it could be made to publish this avowal of its own transcendent individuation.

To be sure, the guidance that was meant to reach the world through me would not in any way become a less authentic witness to eternal truth had I not said one word about my own connection to the spiritual Brotherhood —whose many members form a single body— which also was the source from which Compassion's greatest Mediator used to take his teachings in his day.

Necessity, however, demanded this disclosure. Indeed, it would have meant a constant game of hide and seek, a veritable dance on eggs, had I decided to convey the things I had to say without accounting for my own capacity to form objective judgments—knowing final knowledge through my timeless self—as the reliable prerequisite of all the things I teach.

Too much perplexing darkness that long has blinded human souls is lifted, and its gloom dispersed, by making this disclosure. My personal wish to keep the circumstances of my spiritual background purely to myself, could therefore not be heeded.

As a result, I had to bow to the demands of an accepted inner pledge whose burden I could not be spared.

THE OBLIGATION TO REVEAL their timeless origin is not imposed, however, on all my spiritual

Brothers. Only where eternal love exacts this sacrifice, from which innumerable human souls may benefit, is such a self-disclosure made a Brother's burden.

Who, indeed, would ever willingly expose his being's inmost self, and if it were for all the treasures of the earth, unless he did so in obedience to inexorable spiritual duty?

The insights that my writings bring the present world shall offer light to even the most distant future ages, when all beliefs that now feel threatened by these teachings, or think they may exempt themselves from their demands, will long have ceased to matter.

In the same way as Compassion's greatest Mediator, I, too, am bound to state that I do not "teach on my own authority"—merely as a mortal human being—but what the *Father,* whom I serve in timeless love, has given *me,* my teachings give to *you.*

These teachings are, however, nothing other than objective expositions, conveyed by means of words, of everlasting and eternally immutable realities, whose presence I can enter and experience whenever I desire.

The faculty of lucidly discerning the nature of the one and only absolute Reality remains the sacred heritage of all who are the *Father's* light-begotten *Sons.*

And in this way I teach you, from the fullness of the *Word* even as the *Father* charges me to teach, and so proclaim that you shall find salvation's freedom through the power of celestial love.

Blest are all who will not merely read my words, but let them gain expression in their souls, so that they may shed light upon their readers' lives and make their deeds bear lasting fruit.

A life informed of spiritual deeds will in such readers then awaken highest love; and once consumed by its eternal fire they one day shall attain a radiance without end.

But the attainment of that radiance, enkindled by Primordial Light, remains your highest goal in everlasting life. That you indeed may one day reach this goal, I seek to clear your mind of all debris that clutters up your inner world and keeps your soul in darkness.

It matters little whether you "believe"—or "question"—what I tell you. But if you *act* according to my words and let their spirit guide your steps you shall within yourself *experience* spiritual life. And then you need no longer look for the approval, nor fear the doubt, of searching thoughts your fancy spun within your mind.

I assure you, it is not presumption on my part that causes me to tell you that gaining your approval is not my chief concern.

How you today regard the insights I present—before you have yourself *experienced* spiritual life—is important only because your present judgment either may incline you to be guided by my counsel, or will prevent your following this path.

The truth itself, however, which my words convey will not in any manner either be expanded or diminished by your judgment.

Not your intellect's assumptions, only the celestial form of love that lives within you will ever let you apprehend that truth.

CHAPTER FOUR

ON LOVE'S CREATIVE POWER

Love reveals its origin as a primordial power even in its lower, earthly form; and here already is its nature manifested as creative energy. Followers of very early cults thus came to hope they might unlock the final secrets of love's power even in that lower, earthly form.

Cults devoted to that notion have survived until this day; and error-laden doctrines have lately taken up the most destructive concepts of secret Asian sects, exhumed on gloomy paths, to spread their damage also in the West. Regrettably, it has found wider circulation than the "enlightened" public of the Western world's great cities is likely to suspect.

Ominous destructive energies, released by fiendishly fanaticized Orientals from temple crypts in gloomy night, in this way seek their victims also among non-Orientals.

The foolish hope of gaining "secret powers" and thus to dominate one's fellow mortals who are not equally "initiated" is typically the foremost pander in this quest.

Yet thus beguiled, the wretched victims neither feel that they are merely puppets moved by hidden strings; nor, indeed, do they suspect that their endeavors will drive them toward a goal they hardly would pursue if they foresaw its consequences.

Feeling certain to have found the key that will unlock the final secret of life's mysteries, they listen to the words of self-deluded "adepts" who tell them that they shall discover godlike freedom on this path, while in effect they blithely rush toward the voracious "hounds of the abyss," whose maws already drip from greed to tear their victims' souls to pieces, even as they long since had destroyed the souls of those whom now the unsuspecting pupils honor as empowered "masters" of their diabolically perverted faith.

It is true that, from the dawn of time, the images of phallus and yoni were revered as sacred symbols and, as polar opposites, both signify the holy anchors of earthly life's profoundest mysteries. Nonetheless—whoever here would seek before he has been sought, let him be very careful, lest he confuse the realms he would explore and thus should summon from the deep not the "holy anchors" he desired, but slippery coils of serpents.

There truly is no other realm of occult energies that offers a more copious potential for delusions than does the mystery surrounding sexuality.

To be pitied is the fate of those who think that here they will discover what they seek!

At best they may arouse their mediumistic faculties, which readily will grant them any phantom image that might strengthen their belief, so that enmeshed in self-delusions they deem themselves "like unto gods." Until one day they ruefully discover to their horror, but too late, that they have forfeited their soul's salvation, having listened to the "serpent of the garden."

Whoever finds he has pursued this path should lose no time, but tear himself at once from everything that might attach him to its practice, because the dangers that confront him are immense.

But one who cannot sacrifice, if necessary, everything he may hold dear "for the sake of the kingdom of heaven," truly is unworthy of that "kingdom." Nor, indeed, shall he escape the fate of being cast out "into utter darkness," where he faces, if not permanent destruction, surely aeons of tormenting anguish, fully conscious of his guilt.

All the exalted, often cryptic words that touch upon the mystery enshrouding earthly nature's procreative power and its organs can be truly comprehended only if one knows that the respective energies concealed in this domain will yield themselves, in their profoundly beneficial form, to no one but a Mediator, to one perfected by primordial Light, and purely as an unsought consequence of his perfection in the Spirit.

Needless to say, to release these energies in spiritual ways, which only those are able to effect who have been granted that authority, compares no more to what goes on in certain "esoteric" circles than highly specialized research in chemistry resembles the concoctions of mentally unstable cooks of swill.

Whoever did not reach his spiritual perfection —had been a *master* in the Spirit's world— before his birth in mortal life, should here refrain from searching in whatever form. For what he thinks he might discover he surely will not find; and what he may uncover would only cause him to fall prey to sinister, destructive forces whose hidden nets have captured countless thousands since the dawn of time. Often in their mortal lives for some time still beheld with awe and venerated as authentic "adepts," they would in this way serve the demons that destroyed them as tempting bait to capture other victims.

I do not think I need to make the point that I am quite familiar with all the vaunted "secret methods" that are able to unleash what are mistakenly considered to be "spiritual" energies.

But since I also am familiar with the unhappy fate of those who had unleashed these energies, I am compelled explicitly to warn all those who still are willing to be warned.

"Whoever has ears to hear with, let him hear!"

None to whom this warning is addressed can justly claim I was not clear enough in touching on a subject I would rather not discuss in more detail.

To all of those among you, on the other hand, who would discover light that truly grants illumination and will not make you slaves of occult forces of delusion, which draw on nothing more than traces of your forebears' lives, still preserved within your mortal bodies' cells; to all of you I here will show how love's creative power can manifest itself within you, and may become your own in ways protected from all dangers—by virtue of that timeless revelation of celestial love that fills your souls with living light and with the radiance of a spiritual sun. Even as the lower *earthly* form of love will but enflame your senses in order to preserve your kind, and in its blaze to let you feel that, truly, such a force is also capable of realizing greater things.

Elements of the divine are doubtless present also in love's lower form and can be found in it by those who have already comprehended that both the earthly and the high celestial form of love are ultimately of *one essence* and differ only in the way their nature is made manifest.

But such will not be seeking "occult powers" in love's *earthly* realm. However, when their souls' inherent consciousness pervades their bodies' union, they here may well discern the first sublime reflections of a force that guides them toward love's highest form, where it becomes *celestial*; for here its powers far transcend this mortal life; indeed, reach far beyond the realms of the most distant stars, into the spheres of purest light, of infinite primordial creation, which none can ever enter but the "pure in heart."

STILL, YOU NEED NOT in your mortal life experience *earthly* love in order to attain that selfsame power's highest, its *heavenly* expression.

You certainly should not renounce love's *earthly* form when it would find your heart, inspired by your soul, in a marriage honored as a sacred bond. But if you knew it merely as a means to satisfy desire, then also my advice would be to exercise abstention. Still, I am the last to harbor the illusion that renouncing earthly love is the required price that must be paid to reach one's highest spiritual development.

Even so, you will fare better consciously to sacrifice *one* source of happiness in earthly life, rather than, by gratifying brutish drives, to desecrate the sacred fire.

LOVE'S HIGHEST, ITS *celestial* form can manifest itself within you even in the course of your most ordinary daily work. And some there were in whom its power had awakened, in pure simplicity of heart, while they but labored at a weaver's loom, or humbly ploughed behind their teams, whereas others preached about it all their lives from lofty pulpits, but never knew to find it in themselves.

Even where you feel you are but toiling in some tedious daily chore can love's creative energy reveal itself within you.

More intensely is its presence doubtless felt by all who know their calling lies within the realm of art and who themselves become creators of the forms they feel compelled to bring forth by their spirit.

No masterwork of timeless art has ever been produced on earth without eternal love's creative energy inspiring its creator.

Nonetheless, it would be narrow-minded to presume that only artists are endowed with this creative gift.

There is much work of the most varied kinds to be accomplished in this life on earth where love's creative power must inspire those performing it, albeit in less obvious ways, if they would consecrate their lives' endeavors with enduring worth.

Many an activity quite unrelated to the realm of art can nonetheless, if one regards it from a higher point of view, reveal the same primordial laws, demand the same creative inspiration that also manifests itself within the artist's work; only it is more apparent in the latter.

There is no work of any nature that human beings will perform on earth which love's creative energy could not set free from its confining shackles.

YET IF YOU WOULD encounter the creative power of *celestial* love in its most wondrous revelation you must yourself become the formative "material" its energy can mold.

You shall in vain attempt to find your highest inner form relying merely on your own resources as long as you are not prepared and willing to see your inner self transformed by love's creative power.

Day after day you shall attempt to carve and scrape your inner form in vain as long as you prevent *celestial* love's creative power from sculpting, out of your eternal self, the image of the godhead that is to manifest the Spirit's light: embodied in your being.

Drawing on your own creative energies alone that likeness cannot ever gain its form; however much *celestial* love's creative power has need of also your resources—which love itself bestowed on you—in order to complete its work.

You certainly should not remain inactive; for only constant practice will let your given energies grow strong enough to make them serve as worthy tools of love's creative power in your quest to lend your timeless self enduring form. However, you must not entrust those tools but to the highest mastership of spiritual love if you would see yourself arise in your potential's perfect form.

YET EVEN THEN THERE will be things in your external life that do not always willingly submit to the demands your highest form imposes. Thus, while you live on earth, you need to keep your tools at all times sharp and ready, lest the perfect form you had been granted should once again be lost, leaving but a torso to bear painful witness to a work that had already been accomplished but then again destroyed.

No mortal ever has attained perfection in this present world, through love's creative power, whose highest form had not been threatened by earthly life's forever restless forces of destruction. And if you thought that Luminaries, who mediate eternal Light, could surely not have anything to fear in this respect, I am obliged to tell you that even they, like all who strive to unify their mortal creature life with their eternal being, must be watchful every hour, lest they fall from highest realms of light and, like a star that plunges into the abyss, be shattered and dissolve again into creation's primal elements.

Although in fact extremely rare, such cases nonetheless remain a possibility.

Having fallen from the world of highest light, such a former master then becomes a horrible fanatic of pure evil; a being without conscience who will walk over dead bodies to gain his ends and finds his greatest satisfaction in destroying, wherever he is able, the very works in whose creation he himself had once performed his part.

For anyone who, in the Spirit's world, has been prepared to bear this burden, it thus will always be an undertaking of immeasurable daring when he, of his own free will, accepts the call to unify his timeless spirit's nature with the mortal human creature's life; because the earthly path of such a Mediator is beset by far more numerous and deadly inner perils than is the life of any other mortal.

For that reason you must learn to see that even one who is a Luminary of eternal Light remains a fellow human brother, by no means free of human failings, and thus compelled to struggle, like yourself, if from the conflict between light and darkness he would at last come forth in victory the day his earthly life has reached its end.

You have been taught to worship the radiant Luminary whom we call Compassion's greatest Mediator, as a "God," devoid of sin, incapable of errors causing guilt. Yet this belief has utterly beclouded your sound judgment; indeed, has set you far back into a condition of pitiful dependency, in which all those would gladly keep you chained who only thus are able to enjoy their role as masters of the poverty and serfdom they have laid upon your soul, and as the judges of its fate.

NOT ALL WHO TEACH YOU such mistaken doctrines are aware of what they do.

Most of them indeed believe that they are guiding you toward your salvation, toward happiness and timeless joy.

Today, they are no longer even conscious of the damage done by mortal human arrogance, which is transparent in their actions and has become established practice through the centuries. And so they honestly believe your soul's salvation is in peril the moment you appear to move away from their control and doctrines, because within your heart of hearts you finally began to recognize the errors of their teachings.

Still, you must not make such self-deluded teachers bear the blame for their mistaken doctrines, which the greater part among them hold and offer "in good faith."

Doubtless, they would also guide you well on better paths, if they were to discover such themselves; because, in truth, their work is also motivated, perhaps more often than you think, by the inspired will to bring you help.

But none who truly feels concern for your eternal soul and for its spiritual salvation will forbid you to explore a path that you have found without his help; for well he knows the heavy burden of responsibility his office as a pastor once had laid upon his shoulders.

Only one possessed by pride, who fears to lose his power by your gaining knowledge, will, divested of his armor, unleash at you a flood of words from high upon his pulpit, seeking to persuade you by a thousand reasons to return to the officially restricted pasture of the closed-in fold he holds so dear. The only reason he will not reveal is that which proves his real motive: to keep you firmly where you stood—before the truth whose very source is love was able finally to reach you.

Such a one who fears that he might lose his power is, understandably, beyond the reach of love and its creative energy.

Him you must not follow into the mental labyrinths that he and his companions have skillfully designed to capture anyone attempting to escape their domination. Those who wield such power deem its use delicious; even if, within their heart of hearts, the holders of such might know very well that all their influence rests only in their subjects' being kept from gaining knowledge.

Those who once have tasted the intoxicating thrill of exercising such control will then no longer hear the voice of truth; nor can they any more fulfill eternal truth's inexorably sanctioned spiritual conditions.

Yet do not feel resentful toward even those who are beyond the reach of truth, if you indeed would gain your own self's highest form by letting love's creative energies transform your inner being.

Otherwise, you would create an obstacle and seriously endanger the perfecting of your own eternal form.

You, a reader seeking to discover and experience light, be sure you learn to show compassion to even those who, if they had their will, would gladly hold you captive in the confines of their twilight gloom.

It often was not their own fault that they became what now they are; and thus it is too difficult for most of them courageously to break the fetters which not seldom are the only firm support preventing them from falling into even darker straits; for they are fully conscious, deep within, that only rigid bonds can offer them the hold they need.

Not a few who thus will "blindly lead the blind" regard the common fear of losing access to the source providing for their livelihood as ample reason to continue serving errors they may have recognized themselves and gladly would abandon, if they but knew how else to earn their keep among the souls who have till now sustained their modest sinecure.

Society today may well lament that they, who are no more than sacrificial victims, must now atone for "sins" of long forgotten generations, whose heirs they have become. However, one would merely heap new guilt upon the old if those who rather should be pitied, as being closely fettered mind and soul, were to be held accountable for not yet having cast aside the heavy yoke of ancient times.

Those, by contrast, who still can freely move and use their arms shall one day unexpectedly amaze the world; nor shall even one of them be absent at the time that work is to be done.

Quietly, without disturbing others, they shall prepare and choose the day for breaking free from inner bonds—without committing sacrilege against the sacred shrines and vessels of the past.

Nor shall they tolerate the desecration of a holy site, but will instead rebuild the sanctuary to make it rise anew.

They shall no longer follow teachers who assure them that the great "Anointed One" is found at one place or another, and not a few who boast to have "come in his name" they will divest of fame and of authority.

By their actions they indeed shall not destroy; yet much that had seemed obsolete and of no further use will find itself renewed, because they will at last imbue the ancient form of faith with all the wealth of life its body can contain.

Today one surely cannot yet predict the day when these events are to begin. That such a day will come, however, is as certain as the sunrise that is bound to lift the darkness even of the longest night.

Allow your teachers time to seek; and once they shall have found, or even have been found themselves, they, or their successors, doubtless shall more competently guide you —or your great-grandchildren's children— than they can today.

The best among them will themselves admit they still are only searching for the truth they once believed they had already found when, all consumed with holy zeal, they eagerly embraced the burdens of their office.

Again, you should not think that you could ever find eternal truth's unsullied trace in any other group of seekers here on earth; even where they like to dress up in the threadbare cloaks of ancient mysticism, and assure you, with airs of sibylline profundity, that they alone are guardians of creation's final "secrets."

Doubtless, even here you will find serious minds at work who seek among the hieroglyphs of long since ruined temples for the hidden word that finally might bring them liberation.

Yet knowledgeable sources have long since recognized that also here new methods of inquiry must be found if countless earnest seekers are not to lose themselves among the murky crypts whose tunnels promise "light" at every further turn, yet after endless times of groping in the dark will only plunge the hapless seeker into depths of anguish. Unless, that is, he is content with merely playing an "initiate"; given that, confused and seeing no escape, his vanity is flattered by the trappings of a dignity whose mask allows him to enjoy the trusting faith of the misguided souls that honor him as one who truly has attained the final goal.

Here one also can find others who already search for highly questionable substitutes, because they have no longer any concept of the temple's towering structure, nor of its lofty halls, and thus assume the golden treasure that lies hidden in the sanctuary's inmost shrine is lost beyond recovery.

Eagerly they scour occultism's every cesspool in search of that which the courageous only find upon the snowcapped peaks that tower in the radiant sun.

Yet here as well shall love's creative power in its highest form bring forth a renovation; even though some newly built adjacent halls already show their fundaments eroded by that night-begotten doctrine whose disciples seek the answer to all mysteries of being within love's earthly, mortal creature form.

Those to whom these comments are addressed will doubtless understand me. Others, being not familiar with the subject here discussed may treat my warnings as not concerning them.

The insights that I offer in this book are meant to shed their light on every reader's path, and all are free to search in it for that which best will serve their inner need.

No one's search shall be in vain, and each will find in it the things that speak to him.

In all of them, however, will love's creative energy itself transform to light and life what I was here permitted to convey in writing only to the end of guiding those who at this age abide in darkness to the ancient path of light on which this earthly life can radiantly unfold itself in happiness and joy.

To be sure, there cannot be a harvest unless one first has planted seed. Nor, indeed, may you, to whom I here address myself, expect to gather fruit by merely looking at my words from time to time, but only through your resolutely acting in the spirit of my counsels.

Those who share their lives with me, abiding in the *Father's* love, deem the present age sufficiently prepared to be entrusted with these teachings.

Only since I, too, am conscious of the searching anguish of this age did I consent to put this knowledge into words.

Yet also here I did not write a single sentence that any of my spiritual *Brothers* would not be able to approve. And they alone are capable of judging whether I have met the task that I was given, according to their charge; whether, that is, I have only taught what the eternal *Father* had commanded me to teach.

I alone, however, bear responsibility for every word I write and publish.

May those whom providential guidance—to which they give the name of "chance"—has caused to find the present book allow its words to guide them toward the highest form of timeless love.

May the very light that once had shone upon "the shepherds keeping watch at night," as witnessed in the sacred legend, also reach the hearts of all who in the darkness of the present age are still awake in spirit. And may it, thus, bring peace to all who in these current days of raging conflicts continue to be human beings "of good will"!

Then shall love's creative power teach all those who have awakened how they may lend this life new meaning and new form.

They, however, shall no longer be possessed by the illusion that mankind's spiritual temple cannot be built but from the ruins of demolished shrines; and all shall dedicate themselves to serve that edifice as individual *stones,* once having recognized that life's most sacred sanctuary can be created only out of *living forms.*

In this book I surely left no matter unexamined that you need to know, or knowing which you might find useful even in the smallest way. And where I found its first edition still had left some questions open, they have been answered in sufficient detail in this definitive revision of the work.

My books do not address themselves to starry-eyed enthusiasts who follow any cult or circle seeking signs and wonders; nor to the countless minds to whom reality appears an insubstantial mist, because the only thing they still can apprehend is the continued flicker of the mental images created by the phantoms of their dreams.

The present book, like all my works, is written for mature and sober-minded readers; for individuals who are prepared, by quietly perfecting their own lives, to do their part in spiritually reshaping the structure of a world whose face can only be redeemed by love in its celestial revelation from the disfiguring convulsions that all but caused its features to be frozen in a mask of horror.

Not until the insight has begun to dawn that the external forms of mankind's coexistence on this planet are actively determined by each and every human being's quest for individual perfection and that these forms can be affected from without to only a quite limited degree: not until that day can one be certain to have found the path toward which I seek to guide all those who put their trust in me.

It is the only certain path that leads out of the confusion of the present age and guides one to a higher vantage point, from which one can survey, in clarity, the values that should guide one's earthly life. Nor is there any other path that will allow all those who lost their way to find, within themselves, the timeless peace that every heart which has not wholly turned to stone so ardently desires.

The human mortal's animal belligerence will then no longer be allowed to rage untamed as a destructive force amidst the social bodies of mankind. Instead, this energy will be transformed into a potent spiritual armor that shall enable multitudes of independent individuals to fend off—in themselves—all possible assaults made on their souls by netherwordly powers of this planet. And everyone will wage that battle in the conscious knowledge of the only might that shall triumphantly defeat and conquer every impulse seeking to destroy man's happiness on earth.

REMINDER

"Yet here I must point out again that if one would derive the fullest benefit from studying the books I wrote to show the way into the Spirit, one has to read them in the original; even if this should require learning German.

"Translations can at best provide assistance in helping readers gradually perceive, even through the spirit of a different language, what I convey with the resources of my mother tongue."

From "Answers to Everyone" (1933), *Gleanings*. Bern: Kobersche Verlags-buchhandlung, 1990

Other Works by Bô Yin Râ published in English translation:

Bô Yin Râ: An Introduction to His Works

Contents: Preface. About My Books. Concerning My Name. In My Own Behalf. Essential Distinction. Résumé. Comments on the Cycle <Hortus Conclusus> and the Related Works. Brief Biography of Bô Yin Râ. The Works of Bô Yin Râ.

The Kober Press, 2004, 117 pages, paperback. ISBN 0-915034-10-7

This book presents a summary of the essential features that set the author's works on final things apart from the innumerable publications, old and new, that seek to answer questions which thinking minds have asked in every generation. Traditionally, such answers draw upon beliefs, accepted faith, and speculative thought, culminating in systems of religion and philosophy. Rarely have solutions rested on objective insights into the dynamic structure of reality, embracing both its physical and spiritual dimensions. But in addition to providing such direct descriptions of these aspects of reality, the author's books are helpful guides that let the readers gradually develop their inherent faculties so that they may experience this reality themselves. For readers having sensed the nature of this ultimate experience the concepts "spirit," "soul, "eternal life," and "God" are then no longer merely abstract notions based on hope and faith, but have become realities that form the human being's timeless essence, even as they underlie all aspects of creation.

In the first chapter of this *Introduction* the author discusses the origin and purpose of his books; how they should be used; for whom they are intended, and what their application may accomplish. Here he also stresses that his writings neither are opposed to, nor written to support, any particular religious creed, even though the followers of all persuasions may benefit from what they have to offer to all who seek to know.

The following chapter sheds light on the author's name and explains why his books are published under this spiritual proper name, which is not an arbitrary pseudonym, invented for the purpose of effective self-illumination, but expresses, in phonetic equivalents, the essence of his nature.

In the final chapter he corrects a number of misunderstandings of his books and person, typically prompted by hasty judgments, hearsay, or prejudice. Here he also touches on the common source of all authentic spiritual disclosures and stresses that objective insights into that dimension ought to be distinguished from the subjective mystical visions found in the different forms of religion.

The Book on the Living God

Contents: Word of Guidance. "The Tabernacle of God is with Men." The "Mahatmas" of Theosophy. Meta-Physical Experiences. The Inner Journey. The En-Sof. On Seeking God. On Leading an Active Life. On "Holy Men" and "Sinners." The Hidden Side of Nature. The Secret Temple. Karma. War and Peace. The Unity among Religions. The Will to Find Eternal Light. Mankind's Higher Faculties of Knowing. On Death. On the Spirit's Radiant Substance. The Path toward Perfection. On Everlasting Life. The Spirit's Light Dwells in the East. Faith, Talismans, and Images of God. The Inner Force in Words. A Call from Himavat. Giving Thanks. Epilogue.

The Kober Press, 1991. 333 pages, paperback. ISBN 0-915034-03-4

This work is the central volume of the author's *Enclosed Garden*, a cycle of thirty-two books that let the reader gain a clear conception of the structure, laws, and nature of eternal life, and its reflections here on earth. The present work sheds light on the profound distinction between the various ideas and images of "God" that human faith has molded through the ages —as objects for external worship—and the eternal *spiritual reality*, which human souls are able to experience, even in this present life. How readers may attain this highest of all earthly goals; what they must do, and what avoid; and how their mortal life can be transformed into an integrated part of their eternal being, are topics fully treated in these pages.

What sets this author's works on spiritual life apart from other writings on the subject is their objective clarity, which rests upon direct perception of eternal life and its effects on human life on earth. Such perception is only possible, as he points out, if the observer's *spiritual* senses are as thoroughly developed to perceive realities of timeless life, as earthly senses need to be in order to experience *physical* existence. Given that authentic insights gathered in this way have always been extremely rare, they rank among the most important writings of their time, conveying knowledge of enduring worth that otherwise would not become accessible.

The Book on Life Beyond

Contents: Introduction. The Art of Dying. The Temple of Eternity and the World of Spirit. The Only Absolute Reality. What Should One Do?

The Kober Press, 2002. 161 pages, paperback. ISBN 0-915034-11-5.

This book explains why life "beyond" is not so much a different and wholly other life, but rather the continuation of the self-same life we live on earth. The difference between the two dimensions lies chiefly in the organs of perception through which the same reality of life is individually experienced. On earth we know that life through our mortal senses, in life beyond it is perceived through spiritual faculties, which typically awaken after death. At that transition, the human consciousness, which usually is unprepared for the event, is at a loss and finds itself confused by the beliefs and concepts of its former mortal life. As a result, the new arrival faces certain dangers; for, owing to these mental prejudices, the person is unable to distinguish between perceptions of objective truth and the alluring phantom "heavens" generated by misguided faith on earth.

To help perceptive readers form correct and realistic expectations, that they may one day reach the other shore with confidence and without fear, this book provides trustworthy guidance into spiritual life, its all-pervading structure, laws, and inner nature. Given the unbreakable connection between our actions here on earth and their effects on life beyond, the book advises how this present life may best prepare the reader for the life that is to come.

The Book on Human Nature

Contents: Introduction. The Mystery Enshrouding Male and Female. The Path of the Female. The Path of the Male. Marriage. Children. The Human Being of the Age to Come. Epilogue. A Final Word.

The Kober Press, 2000, 168 pages, paperback, ISBN 0-915034-07-7

Together with *The Book on the Living God* and *The Book on Life Beyond*, *The Book on Human Nature* forms a trilogy containing guidelines toward a new and more objective understanding of both physical and spiritual realities, and of the human being's origin and place within these two dimensions of creation.

The Book on Human Nature at the outset shows the need to draw a clear distinction between the timeless spiritual component present in each mortal human, and the material creature body in which the spiritual essence is embodied during mortal life. The former, indestructible and timeless, owing to its being born of spiritual substance, represents the truly human element in what is known as mortal man. The latter, physical, contingent, and subject to decay and death, is no more than the temporary instrument the spiritual being uses to express itself in physical existence. Given that the spiritual and animal components within human nature manifest inherently discordant aspects of reality, they typically contend for domination of the total individual. Experience shows that in this conflict the animal component with its ruthless drives and instincts clearly proves the stronger.

To help the reader gain a realistic understanding of the human being's spiritual and physical beginnings, by way of concepts more in keeping with humanity's advances in every discipline of natural science, the book explains, to the extent that metaphysical events can be conveyed through language, the timeless origin and source of every human's spiritual descent. It likewise shows that the material organism, now considered mankind's primal ancestor, existed long before it was to serve the spiritual individuation as its earthly tool. In this context the author points out that the traditional creation story, such as it has survived, is not simply an archaic myth, invented at a time that lacked the benefits of modern knowledge, but instead preserves, in lucid images and symbols, a truthful view of actual events. Events, however, that did not happen merely once, at the beginning of creation, but are a process that continues even now, and will recur until this planet can no longer nurture human life.

Even so, the principal intention of the present work, as well as of the author's other expositions of reality, is not so much to offer readers a new, reliable cosmology, but rather to encourage them to rediscover and awaken the spiritual nature in themselves, and thus to live their present and their future life as fully conscious, truly human beings.

The Book on Happiness

Contents: Prelude. Creating Happiness as Moral Duty. "I" and "You". Love. Wealth and Poverty. Money. Optimism. Conclusion.

The Kober Press, 1994. 127 pages, paperback. ISBN 0-915034-04-2.

Sages and philosophers in every age and culture have speculated on the nature, roots, and attributes of happiness, and many theories have sought to analyze this enigmatic subject. In modern times, psychology has joined the search for concrete answers with its own investigations, which frequently arrive at findings that support established views. Still, the real essence of true happiness remains an unsolved riddle.

In contrast to traditional approaches, associating happiness with physical events, the present book points to the spiritual source from which all human happiness derives, both in life on earth and in the life to come. Without awareness of this nonmaterial fundament, one's understanding of true happiness is bound to be deficient.

The author shows that real happiness is neither owing to blind chance, nor a capricious gift of luck, but rather the creation of determined human will. It is an inner state that must be fostered day by day; for real happiness, as it is here defined, is "the contentment that creative human will enjoys in its creation." How that state may be created and sustained, in every aspect of this life, the reader can discover in this book.

The Book on Solace

Contents: On Grief and Finding Solace. Lessons One Can Learn from Grief. On Follies to Avoid. On the Comforting Virtue of Work. On Solace in Bereavement.

The Kober Press, 1996. 126 pages, paperback. ISBN 0-915034-05-0.

In this book the author shows how sorrow, pain, and grief, although inevitable burdens of this present life, can and ought to be confronted and confined within the narrow borders of necessity. Considered from the spiritual perspective, all suffering experienced on this earth is the inexorable consequence of mankind's having willfully abandoned its given state of harmony within the Spirit, a deed that also ruined the perfection of material nature. Although the sum of grief thus brought upon this planet is immense, human beings needlessly expand and heighten its ferocity by foolishly regarding grief as something noble and refined, if not, indeed, a token of God's "grace."

Understanding pain objectively, as a defect confined to physical existence, which, even in exceptional cases, is but an interlude in every mortal's timeless life, allows the reader to perceive its burdens in a clearer light, and thus more patiently to bear it with resolve.

While suffering, through human fault, remains the tragic fate of physical creation, the highest source of solace, which helps the human soul endure its pain and sorrow, continually sends its comfort from the Spirit's world to all who seek it in themselves. How readers may discover and draw solace from that inner source the present book will show them.

The Wisdom of St. John

Contents: Introduction. The Master's Image. The Luminary's Mortal Life. The Aftermath. The Missive. The Authentic Doctrine. The Paraclete. Conclusion.

The Kober Press, 1975. 92 pages, clothbound. ISBN 0-915034-01-8.

This exposition of the Fourth Gospel is not a scholarly analysis discussing the perplexing riddles of this ancient text. It is, instead, a nondogmatic reconstruction of the actual events recorded in that work, whose author wanted to present the truth about the Master's life and teachings; for the image propagated by the missionaries of the new religion often was in conflict with the facts. The present book restores the context of essential portions of the unknown author's secret missive, which the first redactors had corrupted, so that its contents would support the other gospels.

Written by a follower of John, the "beloved disciple," its purpose was to disavow the "miracles" the other records had ascribed to the admired teacher. His record also is unique in that it has preserved the substance of some letters by the Master's hand, addressed to that favorite pupil. Those writings are reflected in the great discourses which set this gospel text apart and lend it its distinctive tone.

Given the historic impact of the man presented in this work, an accurate conception of his life and message will not only benefit believers of the faith established in his name, but also may explain to others what his death in fact accomplished for mankind.

The Meaning of this Life

Contents: A Call to the Lost. The Iniquity of the Fathers. The Highest Goal. The "Evil" Individual. Summons from the World of Light. The Benefits of Silence. Truth and Verities. Conclusion.

The Kober Press, 1998, 126 pages, paperback. ISBN 0-915034-06-9.

This book addresses the most common questions people tend to ask at times when circumstances in their daily lives awaken their awareness of the many unsolved riddles that surround the human being here on earth. To be sure, philosophy and teachings of religion have offered answers to such questions through the ages, but as these often draw on speculation, or require blind belief, they can no longer truly satisfy the searching mind of our time.

It is against this background that the present book will guide its readers to a firmer ground of understanding, resting on objective insights and experience. From this solid vantage, readers may survey their own existence and its purpose with assurance.

As this book explains, the key to comprehending the meaning of this present life is, first, the insight that this life is but the consequence of causes in the Spirit's world and, thus, has of itself no meaning other than that fact. And, secondly, the recognition that material life is ultimately meaningless if human beings fail to give it meaning: by virtue of pursuing goals whose blessings shall endure. The nature of the highest goal that mortals can pursue provides the substance also of the present book.

Spirit and Form

Contents: The Question. Outer World and Inner Life. At Home and at Work. Forming One's Joy. Forming One's Grief. The Art of Living Mortal Life.

The Kober Press, 2000. 108 pages, paperback. ISBN 0-915034-07-7

The underlying lesson of this book is that all life in the domain of spiritual reality, from the highest to the lowest spheres, reveals itself as lucid order, form, and structure. Spirit, the all-sustaining radiant *substance* of creation, is in itself the final source and pattern of all perfect form throughout its infinite dimensions. Nothing, therefore, can exist within, or find admittance to, the Spirit's inner worlds that is devoid of the perfection, harmony, and structure necessarily prevailing in these spheres.

Given that this present life is meant to serve the human being as an effective preparation for regaining the experience of spiritual reality, this life must needs be lived in ways that are consistent with the principles that govern spiritual reality; in other words, ought to be lived according to the structure, laws, and inner forms of that reality. To show the reader how this present life receives enduring form, which then is able to survive this mortal state, the book sheds light on crucial aspects of this physical existence and advises how these may be formed to serve one's spiritual pursuits.

Worlds of Spirit
A Sequence of Cosmic Perspectives

Contents: Preface. The Ascent. The Return. Reviews of Creation. Epilogue.

Illustrations: *Emanation. In Principio erat Verbum. Lux in Tenebris. Te Deum Laudamus. Space and Time. Primal - Generation. Seeds of Future Worlds. Emerging Worlds. Birth of the External Cosmos. Labyrinth. Desire for External Form. Astral Luminescence. Sodom. Inferno. De Profundis. Revelation. Illumination. Fulfillment. Victory. Himavat.*

The Kober Press, 2002. 96 pages, 20 full-color illustrations, hardcover. ISBN 0-915034-09-3.

If all the books of Bô Yin Râ, objectively considered, are unparalleled in the extensive literature on subjects touching final things—in that their author did not publish speculations based on faith or thought, but gave the reader fact-based insights into spiritual reality—the volume *Worlds of Spirit* occupies a special place even among these thirty-two unprecedented works; for in this book he integrated twenty reproductions of his paintings, representing *spiritual perspectives*, to illustrate selected aspects of his text.

While the works of the *Hortus Conclusus* cycle constitute the first authentic, comprehensive exposition of metaphysical realities, the paintings in this volume represent, in turn, the first objective visual renditions of spiritual dimensions in their dynamic figurations, colors, and inherent structure. Together with the written word—the book describes events experienced and perceived by an awakened human spirit—the images are meant to offer readers lucid concepts of nonphysical existence, and thereby to assist them in developing their own perceptive faculties.

THE
KOBER
PRESS

Lightning Source UK Ltd.
Milton Keynes UK
UKHW012003090322
399819UK00002B/634